FAMILY MINISTRY ESSENTIALS: AN ORANGE STRATEGY GUIDE

Family Ministry Essentials:
An Orange Strategy Guide

Published by Orange, a division of The reThink Group, Inc.
5870 Charlotte Lane, Suite 300
Cumming, GA 30040 U.S.A.

Visit our website at www.thinkorange.com for more resources like these.

ISBN: 978-1-63570-191-3

©2022 The reThink Group, Inc.

Developed by Reggie Joiner, Kristen Ivy, and the Orange Team
Lead Editors: Afton Phillips, Mike Jeffries
Lead Designer: Ashley Shugart
Project Manager: Brian Sharp

Printed in the United States of America

First Edition 2022

1 2 3 4 5 6 7 8 9 10

4/12/22

FAMILY MINISTRY ESSENTIALS: AN ORANGE STRATEGY GUIDE

 orange

WHO WE ARE

We are a team of ministry leaders, educators, researchers, counselors, writers, editors, artists, technicians, directors, musicians, and producers all committed to supporting churches and families as they nurture the faith and future of the next generation.

We are content and experience creators.

We are a non-profit organization that writes over a million words a month.

We produce over 400 videos and 20 national training events each year.

7

We target 7 audiences:

→ Preschoolers
→ Elementary Kids
→ Middle Schoolers
→ High Schoolers
→ Church Staff
→ Volunteers
→ Parents

We are leaders who represent over 80 different Christian denominations.

The work we do supports evangelical, mainline, orthodox, and ecumenical churches who are passionate about . . .

1. The message and mission of the Gospel
2. The faith and future of the Next Generation

We believe you are probably more Orange than you may realize. Chances are you are already Orange even if you have never attended an Orange event or used Orange as a resource. Here's a quick Orange pop quiz to test your Orange-ness:

Do you believe . . .

→ mixing red and yellow creates the color orange?
→ the home and church can influence a child's faith?
→ Jesus said the greatest commandment is to love God?
→ personal faith has the potential to impact someone's future?
→ leaders and parents need an intentional strategy to disciple kids and teenagers?

How did you do? If your answer to most of the above was yes, you are already thinking Orange. Here are a few more.

Do you think . . .

→ getting leaders and volunteers to work as a team is mission critical?
→ how you say what you say to kids and teenagers really does matter?

- most parents want to do the best job possible at raising their kids?
- it takes consistent and caring relationships to "make disciples?"
- influencing kids and students to serve others will affect their faith?

Give yourself 10 points for each answer. This obviously isn't a test you pass or fail. It's just to see how Orange you really think. If you agree with us about most of these issues then you are thinking Orange. Even if this is as far as you read, we'll choose to believe we are on the same team.

Being Orange doesn't mean you have to agree with us about everything we say or do. We actually hope you don't. It's how we learn. Our team at Orange doesn't agree with each other about everything either. If we did, we wouldn't need each other to grow.

Even if you have an aversion to the hue of Orange because it's the color of your rival football team, or it clashes with your skin tone, we hope you will keep thinking about Orange concepts. That's why we hope you will consider championing and collaborating about some of the ideas in this guide. There are important conversations we need to have about how we influence the faith and character of the next generation.

We're glad the color Orange is everywhere. It's in your groceries when you buy tangerines, carrots, sweet potatoes, and Goldfish crackers. It's on billboards with some of your favorite brands like Nike, Home Depot, and Dunkin' Donuts. Orange is even woven into nature.

God put in the rainbow, painted it in the sunsets, and gave us pumpkins to make jack-o-lanterns (or pumpkin pie). We love the fact that the color orange can symbolize safety, health, and change.

Orange just seems like the right color to remind us of the potential of an effective family ministry strategy. The color clearly emphasizes that two things working together can result in a third, more vibrant outcome. Think about it this way . . .

THE ORANGE PHILOSOPHY

Two combined influences can make a greater impact than just two influences.

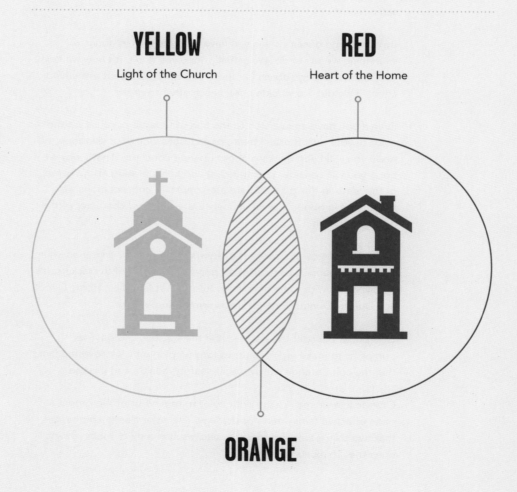

YELLOW

Light of the Church

RED

Heart of the Home

ORANGE

- Yellow can only do what yellow can do.
- Red can only do what red can do.
- But when red and yellow join forces, you get **orange**.

We hope from now on whenever you see the color orange it will remind you that "two combined influences can make a greater impact than just two influences."

We think that "Orange is the new Orange" because it keeps changing—just like your kids ministry, youth ministry, or family ministry. So, let's unpack a little more about the Orange strategy.

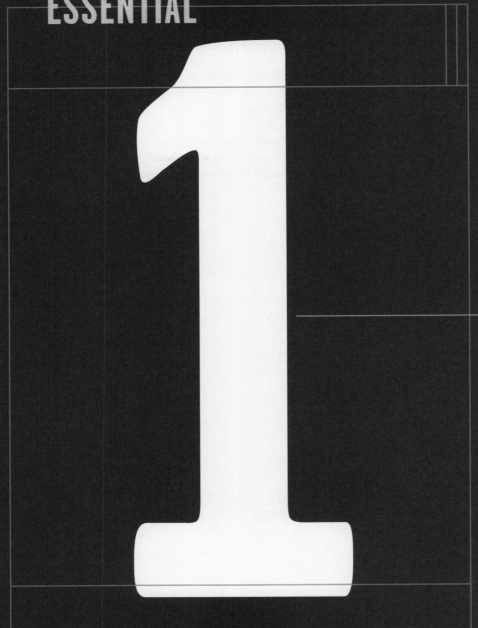

ESSENTIAL

CLARIFY A STRATEGY TO INFLUENCE THE FAITH AND FUTURE OF THE NEXT GENERATION

13

Words are important to us as an organization. There are significant terms in this first essential that we should highlight.

FAITH AND FUTURE

We think leading kids and teenagers to follow Jesus will impact their future.

Jesus was clear when He said, "I have come that you might have life and live more fully." Jesus didn't promise a life of happiness or prosperity. Instead, He invited every generation to follow Him into a life of meaning and purpose. Jesus promised God's love and Spirit would be present every day, no matter what. That's why we want to influence those who influence a kid or teenager's faith. Faith has the potential to impact someone's future because it actually shapes their sense of identity, belonging, and purpose.

THE STRATEGY

Throughout this guide we will use the word "strategy" a lot. A strategy is simply **"a plan of action with an end in mind."** A strategy assumes that we pre-decide what we hope kids will become spiritually. The idea of strategy suggests that we think in terms of steps, not just programs, to keep kids and teenagers moving in a positive direction in their relationship with Jesus. An effective strategy also has the potential to align leaders to move in the same direction and to increase the momentum of an organization. As we get started unpacking the Orange strategy, let's start with a simple visual.

THE INFLUENCES

When you take the light of the church (yellow) and combine it with the love of a family (red) you increase the potential to influence a kid's life.

CHURCH (LIGHT) + HOME (LOVE)
= GREATER IMPACT

Remember, two combined influences, the home and the church, will have more influence together than if they function as two separate influences.

There are two truths that will always be true, even though they may seem to contradict each other:

1. No one has more potential to influence a child than a parent. Whoever has the role of parent, foster parent, stepparent, adoptive parent, or guardian will have more potential to know and influence the kids in their home than any other leaders. Time and proximity will give them an advantage over other adults to make sure a child grows up with a sense of identity and belonging. Whether it is positive or negative, a parent will always tend to have more influence in the life of their child.

TWO COMBINED INFLUENCES

CHURCH

Light

+

HOME

Heart

= GREATER IMPACT

2. A parent is not the only influence a child needs.
Most adults in the parental role realize that kids need other influences. The greatest gift any church can give a family is another adult who will positively impact the faith and future of their children. That's why it's important to develop leaders who show up for kids and partner with parents at the same time. One of the most important things you can do as a family ministry leader is to recognize that the most important work you do is influence parents and leaders to keep influencing the next generation. Here's another way of saying it to make sure we don't miss the idea.

We need to be intentional about clarifying our strategy to influence those who influence the next generation. There's a tendency for any ministry to default to a random approach. We finish a series, host an event, or start a program *then* work on figuring out what to do next. While it's definitely important to evaluate what you did and are doing, your ministry programming and activity needs to be measured against something. A strategy statement can become a compass that gives you a baseline to evaluate everything you do. Here's the one we use at Orange as an example. This is basically a one-sentence description of what we want to help every church do.

> Influence **leaders** and **parents**
> to create **community** around a timeless **message**
> that mobilizes the next generation
> to Love God and **serve** others.

Obviously, everything we want to help you do is not detailed in this one sentence. This phrase doesn't explain the timeless message of the Gospel, clarify what creates authentic community, introduce child-development principles, list goals for parents, or give advice to teenagers about proper use of mobile devices. However, a carefully worded sentence can provide categories to help you determine how to organized a detailed plan.

A good strategy statement reflects the vision and values of an organization. It is the simplest reminder of what you are actually trying to do every week. It is also the basis of why and how you plan to accomplish your ultimate end in mind. This one phrase impacts every resource, event, curriculum, partnership, and meeting we do at Orange. Most important, our strategy statement represents what we want to help churches do to shape the faith and character of kids and teenagers. In this sentence the values are easily identifiable:

➡ Leaders
➡ Message
➡ Parents
➡ Community
➡ Service

Further clarifying these values can help us develop a more robust ministry plan. They can influence us to ask the right questions.

How are we actually doing at . . .
➡ working together as **leaders**?
➡ designing experiences that enhance our **message**?
➡ helping **parents** become more effective at home?
➡ creating **community** where volunteers show up consistently?
➡ providing meaningful opportunities for students to **serve**?

INFLUENCE LEADERS AND PARENTS TO CREATE COMMUNITY AROUND A TIMELESS MESSAGE THAT MOBILIZES THE NEXT GENERATION TO **LOVE** GOD AND SERVE OTHERS

THE FIVE VALUES OF ORANGE

Over the years we have solidified what we consider to be Five Core Values that are shared by most churches regardless of size, style, or denomination.

There's nothing really new here. Smarter leaders than us have been talking about a lot of these ideas for decades. We just established a list to help us organize and improve how we do ministry. Most questions that leaders ask us relate to one of these five ideas.

Value No. 1

ALIGN LEADERS

AROUND A COMMON STRATEGY AND COMMON VALUES

The secret to momentum in football, or any sport for that matter, has less to do with talent, and more to do with how the team plays together. You can have the most talented players in the world, and still lose a game simply because the team isn't working together to move the ball down the field.

Remember this principle:
You don't have to work at getting misaligned.
It just happens.
Over time.
On every team.

But you do have to work at alignment.
It doesn't just happen.
Alignment requires intentionality.

Alignment is what you do when you balance your tires after so many miles. If you align them right, you get better fuel economy and a smoother ride. You need to do the same in your ministry. From time to time you need to stop, see how everyone is working together, realign, and go again.

We all know the fallout of not working together as a team.

If you're the youth pastor and you don't get on the same page as the children's pastor—how can you expect a parent who may have kids in both your ministries to get on the same page with your team?

If your volunteers aren't working together in a synchronized way, how can you expect kids or teenagers not to get confused?

If your messaging isn't connected by a similar strategy, how can you avoid creating competing voices and competing messages canceling each other out?

Think about it this way . . .

COMMON STRATEGY + COMMON VALUES
= ALIGNMENT

Having a common strategy and values doesn't mean you agree about everything. Actually, it means that you can have healthy debates about some things, because you agree about the most important things.

In the early days of Orange, we actually used the phrase, "Integrate your strategy." It referred to the importance of having a comprehensive plan that connected every age group. In a ministry culture where kids and youth leaders tend to work in silos, we challenged that paradigm.

Our goal is to get those who lead the preschool, elementary, middle school, and high school strategies to work together on purpose. In the book *It's Just a Phase, So Don't Miss It* we explain why those who work with the next generation should be specialists and generalists.

As a specialist you have to understand the unique needs and aspects of your specific phase or age group.

UNALIGNED VS. ALIGNED LEADERS

UNALIGNED LEADERS

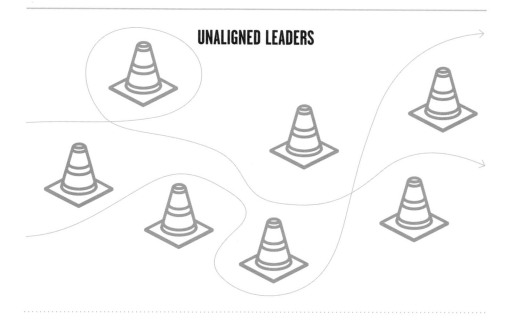

ALIGNED LEADERS

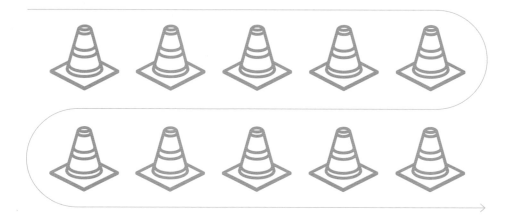

25

As a generalist you have to understand how every other age group is connected to what you do.

When every age group leader begins to value every other age group leader, things will dramatically change in your church:
- ➡ Staff culture and meeting structure will improve.
- ➡ Curriculums will be built around a comprehensive plan.
- ➡ Parents will trust consistent and clear communication.
- ➡ Volunteers will value other volunteers.
- ➡ Serving each other will become a priority.

A good strategy starts by aligning leaders.

Value No. 2

REFINE THE MESSAGE

TO CREATE ENGAGING, RELEVANT, AND MEMORABLE EXPERIENCES

When you really look at the facts, you'll see that most kids and teenagers will show up at your church less than 50% of the time. That means, for example, you will have about 25 hours this year to actually invest in the life of a middle schooler.

Thirty percent of those 25 hours will be spent . . .
trying to find the room
interacting in games
updating their social media
and saying bye to each other as they leave

So, your time with them is limited. Of course, you can hopefully add a retreat, some digital messaging, and maybe food to get them to stay longer. But here's something else to know about that same middle schooler this year:

- → They will spend 200 hours studying math.
- → They will watch 500 hours of TV.
- → They will look at their smart devices for 900 hours.

Realistically, you have somewhere between 20 and 40 hours with them this year.

That's not a lot of time to explain to the average kid or teenager everything they need to know about God, Jesus, faith, forgiveness, and life. So somewhere along the way, you have to make some choices about how you are going to prioritize what you teach.

Are you going to teach them chronologically through the Bible?
Are you going to explain to them the 14 doctrinal statements of your denomination?
Are you going to teach them verse by verse through the book of Habakkuk?
Are you going to amplify whatever your lead pastor just talked about on Sunday morning?

You have 40 hours in a given year to influence the middle schoolers who keep coming back to your church every week, and you are one of the people responsible for their spiritual growth.

So, if you are going to refine your message, you will have to begin by prioritizing which truths are most important.

That's why . . .
you will need to refine the message to **say what matters most**.

We are simply suggesting that it's wise to decide ahead of time the essential truths that you want kids to understand at the end of this year. If your goal is to try to teach them everything, then they may miss the most important things. That's why we create a scope and cycle that prioritizes core insights and recycles them creatively at every phase of a kid's life. But we'll come back to that later.

When you refine the message you learn to **say what matters so it matters**.

As Christian educators and teachers we need to remember that we are stewards of Biblical truths that have life-changing potential. The problem in many churches is not that they don't teach truth, but it's that they don't teach truth in a way that matters to their audience.

Just remember, what you teach doesn't matter simply because it's true. It matters when you make it matter to your audience.

Okay wait.
Don't take this out of context.

Are we saying truth doesn't matter?
No. Of course truth matters.

But . . .
if you don't engage the interests of kids,
they may not hear truth.

if you don't show how truth is relevant to who they are,
they may not embrace truth.

if you don't allow kids to experience for themselves,
they may not remember truth.

That's why we should craft our words carefully, study our audiences diligently, and arrange every experience strategically.

We want to help leaders and volunteers take kids or teenagers through a journey each week so they can understand how the good news of God's story intersects with their personal story. Although God's story is the same, every age group is unique in how they understand and respond to that good news.

That's why at Orange we often say, "Don't teach the Bible to kids, instead teach kids the Bible." If you hope to translate the essence of Scripture to the heart of a kid or teenager, you need to understand how they are wired. That's why we believe that it's important to keep the tensions alive if you want to make an impact with how you teach.

Here are just a few tensions that you will have to manage:

→ **The tension between *truth* and *relevance.***
   Yes, timeless truth is always relevant, but relevance is defined

A CHURCH'S INFLUENCE

40 HOURS
PER YEAR

THE AVERAGE CHURCH
HAS 40 HOURS OF
POTENTIAL INFLUENCE

as "connecting to the matter at hand." If anyone doesn't understand how a truth connects to their everyday life then it may be dismissed as irrelevant. It's critical to apply what is true to their everyday world.

→ **There is a tension between *theology* and child *development*.**
The issues kids face at every phase aren't simply felt needs; they are defining issues that shape their identity. Kids and teenagers are constantly changing morally, culturally, spiritually, mentally, physically, and emotionally. That's why it's important to communicate in a way that leverages where they are developmentally.

→ **There is a tension between *teaching* and *experience*.**
If you were to ask most kids what they remember being taught when they were young, they will make a confession: Not much. At least they don't usually remember words. They can sometimes recall concepts. They can always remember how someone made them feel and what they experienced. That's why it's important to create experiences and even service opportunities that reinforce messaging.

When we refine the message, it simply means we will always keep improving how we create and communicate timeless content for the sake of someone's faith.

Value No. 3

ENGAGE EVERY PARENT

TO BE THE PARENT THEY WANT TO BE

Let's go back to our math. We have calculated that the average ministry leader gets less than 40 hours in a given year to impact the life of a kid or teenager. Let's contrast that with the average guardian or parent. It's a staggering difference. The average parent will have up to 3,000 potential hours to influence their kids and teenagers.

By default, parents have the advantage of time and proximity over any other adult when it comes to influencing their own kids. When you look at the 40 hours you have in contrast to the 3,000 hours parents have, it makes logical sense to partner with parents. If you want to make a difference and have a lasting impact on the life of a kid, you need to think in terms of how to engage parents.

What do we mean by *engage*?

Years ago, we did a national survey of ministry leaders and asked them to describe what it looked like to help parents win. All of the ideas we collected fell into one of two categories.

We help parents win when they become . . .
1. more intentional at home.
2. more connected to a community.

So, what if we start by engaging every parent to do those two things? If your strategy actually helps parents connect to relationships, that will support them to be the parent they want to be in their home.

When we say every parent, we mean every human who has a parental role:

- → Every unmarried parent
- → Every single parent
- → Every divorced parent
- → Every adoptive parent
- → Every foster parent
- → Every stepparent
- → Every grandparent
- → Every guardian
- → Every parent with a child with special needs
- → Every parent who comes on Sunday
- → Every parent who stays home on Sunday

Sure. We know you can't really engage every parent. It's literally impossible. **But when you try to do what's impossible, you will do more than you would have done.**

"Every" suggests that you try to develop empathy for an individual parent's situation.

"Every" implies you should build relationships with parents who are not like you.

"Every" requires you to think about the parents who are not there on Sunday.

If you're going to engage every parent, then start by creating a culture where every parent and volunteer in your church chooses to believe in every parent. Sure, we know some parents who are not good parents, but what if we decided not to let the exceptions become the focus? What if we simply choose to keep believing in every parent's potential?

POTENTIAL INFLUENCE IN A YEAR

40
HOURS

3,000
HOURS

THE CHURCH
HAS 40 HOURS OF
POTENTIAL INFLUENCE

THE AVERAGE PARENT
HAS 3,000 HOURS OF
POTENTIAL INFLUENCE

By the way, if you want parents to change the way they see your church, you may need to change the way your church sees parents.

So if we choose to lead those around us to believe . . .

Every parent wants to be a better parent
> . . . then maybe parents will see the potential we see in them.

Every parent wants their kids to have a better future
> . . . then maybe we can bridge a gap to show parents how faith affects a kid's future.

Every parent will do something more
> . . . then maybe we could cue parents with ideas that actually help them.

Every parent feels responsible for the faith and character of their kids
> . . . then maybe parents will partner with us to build a better strategy.

Every parent knows something about parenting
> . . . then maybe we could actually learn principles and ideas from every parent that can help every other parent and our ministry.

Every parent has more potential to influence their kids than anyone else
> . . . then maybe we would remember why we should keep engaging every parent.

The reason this posture toward every parent is so important is because if parents believe we trust them, they will tend to trust us.

Besides, **what happens at home is more important than what happens at church.**

Value No. 4

ELEVATE COMMUNITY

SO RELATIONSHIPS ARE A PRIORITY

At Orange we champion two strategic
ideas about spiritual influence.

1. No one has more potential to influence
   a child than their parent.

2. A parent is not the only influence a child needs.

That's why we believe one of the most important things any church
can give a family is to put another adult in the life of their kid or
teenager. The mission of the Church is clear. We're supposed to do
what Jesus did. Show up in the lives of others so they can see God.
Engage a generation to follow Jesus, so they will live fully and forever.

That's why the work of every church is so critical. We are called to do
more than simply make a presentation of the Gospel. We are called
to engage in the messiness of humanity because of the Gospel. We
are compelled by the Spirit of Christ to show the world that God
loves them by the way we love them. The fact is, the church is one of
the most divinely strategic organizations that exists.

But when or if a church fails to make relationships a priority,
it takes a huge risk. It's easy to . . .
- build platforms instead of a community.
- create an audience instead of disciples.
- fuel doctrinal debate instead of an everyday faith.

41

God wired each person's faith to be shaped and influenced by a faith community. It's why Jesus introduced the idea of "ecclesia" or a gathering of believers. Regardless of the style or size of any church, the greatest asset the church has to build faith in the next generation is not a Bible study, a worship band, facilities, or a budget. **The most valuable resources any church has to help people see God are the people in the church who know God.** And if we hope to help a generation of kids and teenagers know God, then we have to be strategic about how we connect them to leaders and a community of believers who also believes in them.

That's why we think ministries should consider designing curriculums around a model that makes small groups and relationships a priority. We are convinced that recruiting and developing volunteers to invest consistently in the lives of kids is one of the most important things a church can do. **Kids need to be known by someone before they feel like they actually belong somewhere.** And many of them need to belong before they will ever believe. So, what if our curriculums are organized to include small group discussions or activities to help leaders become intentional about building community?

Leaders who connect with kids in a SMALL group over time have the potential to make a BIG impact on their faith.

We believe every kid and teenager needs a small community or circle of consistent friends and leaders. A small group circle is not the same as a class, a club, or a curriculum. We actually call this idea "leading small." When you lead small, you realize that what you do for a few will always have more potential than what you do for many. When you lead small, you simply make a choice to invest strategically in the lives of a few over time so you can help them build an authentic faith.

The best way to help kids know God is to connect them with someone who knows God.

WHAT YOU
DO FOR A FEW
WILL ALWAYS HAVE
MORE POTENTIAL
THAN WHAT YOU
DO FOR MANY.

Value No. 5

INFLUENCE
SERVICE

AS AN INTEGRAL PART
OF DISCIPLESHIP

Core to our philosophy is the belief that spiritual formation is connected to the act of serving. Something unique happens in a kid or teenagers' life when they serve God by serving others. Stated another way, there is an integral link between loving God and loving others. When we don't help kids make a practical investment of their time and energy to experience what God can do through them, they don't grow spiritually.

This is an important principle to understand in the home and church because it requires an intentional shift in how we do ministry as kids and teenagers transition into adulthood. Too many church programs think kids should sit and listen instead of experiencing hands-on ministry.

As churches we need to remember that there is a critical difference in doing ministry *for* kids and doing ministry *with* kids. That's why we think Sunday should never become merely a spectator sport where kids are encouraged to sit on the sidelines. If kids or teenagers never experience the thrill of actually playing in the game they can grow up and grow out of church. It's easier for kids to get over what you say than it is for them to get over what God does through them.

As important as it is to teach timeless truth, it's also important to remember that faith doesn't simply grow because we know more; it grows when we serve more. A curriculum that incorporates a balance of learning with relevant experience and ministry opportunities is much more likely to encourage students to become responsible for their own spiritual maturity and development.

As you observe the stages of development from preschool to college, the need to experience ministry becomes more intense as kids get older. One of the best ways to convince a child or teen they are significant is to give them something significant to do. That's why in the Orange strategy, small group leaders and parents are trained to enlist and encourage kids to serve consistently. We also think making service a priority for kids and teenagers can have a contagious effect throughout the church culture.

We're not suggesting these are the only five values a ministry should champion, but our experience over the last decade indicates these values are timeless. They can play an integral part in any ministry.

IF YOU WANT KIDS

OR TEENAGERS TO

FEEL SIGNIFICANT

GIVE THEM SOMETHING

SIGNIFICANT TO DO.

47

ESSENTIAL

2

KEEP GOING BACK TO WHY SO YOU CAN REIMAGINE HOW TO DO WHAT YOU DO

49

One of the first steps to managing change is to draw clear lines between "why" and "how" you do what you do.

"WHY" AND "HOW"

The key to building a relevant and engaging family ministry is how you respond to change. Anyone who works with kids and teenagers understands how fast things are changing in the context of their lives and culture.

"Why" represents the values of your ministry that you should keep coming back to when you evaluate your ministry. They typically don't change, but provide a basis for your ongoing strategy.
"How" represents the specific programs, structures, roles, and innovations that determine what you actually do each week.

How you organize kids into small groups
How you assign roles to volunteers
How you promote and teach a new series

How you define your job description
How you resource parents to have conversations

Stated another way . . .

VALUES ARE TIMELESS.
INNOVATIONS ARE TEMPORARY.

Sometimes conflict happens in churches because people get confused between what is temporary and what is timeless. Think about some of the common arguments or debates that have happened in churches over years around . . .

➡ styles of music.
➡ Sunday-morning schedules.
➡ types of preaching.

The point is, if your team agrees on what is timeless they will feel more free to debate what is temporary.

So, let's go back to the values stated in the first section and remember why these concepts can go in the timeless category.

Leadership will always be essential for teams to have direction.
Messaging will always matter if you want to inspire change.
Parents will always have more influence in a kid's everyday life.
Community or belonging will always be a core need of every person.
Service will always have the potential to ignite faith and significance in anyone.

Although these core values will never change, the *shape* of them will need to change. How you effectively accomplish each of these ideas will primarily be influenced by three things.

1. Life stage
2. Culture
3. Crisis

These three factors will shape how you lead, how you teach, how you partner with parents, how you develop volunteers, and how you serve the community.

Creating a culture of change has the best potential to highlight what never changes. Change never compromises your values, it reinforces them. Good innovation is a result of frequently adjusting your "how" to accomplish your "why." As a leader, some of your most important conversations will be to draw a line of distinction between what is timeless and what is temporary. There is tremendous focus and freedom as a team when everyone in the room is anchored to the "why" as they debate the "how."

For example, think about how these values could potentially impact your job description.

JOB DESCRIPTIONS

When you think in terms of the timeless values of a family ministry and apply them to the actual job description of a youth or kids pastor, it can have a ripple effect throughout your organization.

There are a lot of people who have a description of what a kid or youth pastor actually does in their mind:
➡ Your church
➡ Your pastors
➡ Your volunteers
➡ Your parents
➡ Your teenagers
➡ Your kids

So, clarifying what you do for everyone around these values will actually highlight what is timeless in your ministry.

Since there are already multiple people carrying around pictures of what they think your role looks like, you have a chance to clarify it for everyone. It's possible that when you clarify it, they will still try to conform your role to the image of their picture.

That's why one of the most important things you can do for everyone is to clarify your role.

Clarifying your role as a leader actually has the potential to affect everything else in your organization.

- How you recruit volunteers
- How you spend budget
- How you lead meetings
- How you hire staff
- How you evaluate success

But what if we re-write these values to help you accomplish your job? When we work with kid and youth pastors in developing their job description, we always start with this list. Take a look at the following chart to see how establishing timeless values can help you design a practical job description. You can download a free editable version at OrangeLeaders.com. But the point is to anchor what you do to what is timeless. Then, explain what you do so you can start measuring it. It might look like this:

ALIGN LEADERS

To work together around a common strategy, values, and language:
- Champion vision and values of kid or youth ministry throughout church
- Facilitate effective meetings to collaborate with key leaders in your organization
- Manage budget and resources needed to make kids and youth ministry successful

REFINE THE MESSAGE

To create engaging, relevant and memorable experiences
- Produce strategic experiences to be relevant and engaging
- Design a scope and cycle that prioritizes core messages
- Develop and improve a diverse team to communicate and lead experiences

ELEVATE COMMUNITY

So relationships are a priority
- ➡ Recruit and develop volunteers to lead teenagers in weekly small groups
- ➡ Implement a system to recruit and train small group leaders
- ➡ Manage group structure to connect kids and teenagers relationally with peers and leaders

ENGAGE EVERY PARENT

To be the parent they want to be
- ➡ Design strategic opportunities to help every parent stay connected
- ➡ Provide resources and experiences that help parents win with their own kids
- ➡ Leverage digital strategies to keep parents inspired and informed

INFLUENCE SERVICE

As an integral part of discipleship
- ➡ Recruit and develop students as volunteers in various ministries
- ➡ Train adult leaders to co-lead with teenagers
- ➡ Partner with community organizations to engage families to serve

YOUR JOB DESCRIPTION: WHY TO HOW

ALIGN LEADERS

How do you do meetings and measure success?

REFINE THE MESSAGE

How do you improve weekly experiences?

ELEVATE COMMUNITY

How do you develop small group leaders and volunteers?

ENGAGE EVERY PARENT

How do you communicate and connect to parents?

INFLUENCE SERVICE

How do you create consistent serving opportunities for families, kids, and youth?

WEEKLY EXPERIENCES

We also think the curriculum you use every Sunday should actually be a catalyst for improving your overall strategy. Think about it this way.

What if your weekly content and message . . .
- ➡ prioritized the core issues that Jesus said were most important?
- ➡ appealed to the image of God in every person?
- ➡ consistently focused on why kids should reflect and respond to the character of God?
- ➡ clearly showed a generation how following Jesus will affect their future?
- ➡ positioned Sunday as a catalyst for an everyday faith?

What if the experience you create for kids and teenagers this Sunday . . .
- ➡ reflected a comprehensive plan that is recycled from birth to adulthood?
- ➡ co-operated with the unique rhythms that happen within a community's calendar?
- ➡ leveraged an understanding of key child-development issues?
- ➡ solidified truth by connecting teaching to a consistent small group experience?
- ➡ inspired them with a wider range of diverse voices and engaging technology?

What if the curriculum implemented at your church . . .
- ➡ trained your leaders and volunteers as they used it?
- ➡ included seasoned practitioners who would coach your teams?
- ➡ maintained its quality regardless of the size of a staff or church?
- ➡ made it easier for those who don't go to church to feel welcomed by the church?

What if what happens at Sunday School for kids and teenagers . . .
- ➡ included a clear plan and tools so any parent could partner with you?
- ➡ created a common language to get every parent and leader on the same page?

- could be synchronized with other initiatives that happen outside of Sunday?
- mobilized a culture of service throughout your organization?

Then your curriculum would be more than just curriculum, and we are back to the idea of strategy.

If you only have 40 hours—at best—with some kids, then make every hour count. Our curriculum weaves music, large group scripts, small group discussions, video presentations, and activities together to reinforce a bottom line each week. So, kids and teenagers can walk away and remember what they learned. Every principle and story connects to at least one of nine core insights to help them grow in their relationship with Jesus. (We'll unpack those core insights in chapter 3.)

The following section explains the seven segments that Orange features to build their weekly experience for kids and youth. Hopefully you can see the same five timeless values reflected in the programming. It illustrates how the "why" translates into "how."

SEVEN SEGMENTS OF A WEEKLY EXPERIENCE

Whether you know it or not, every time you create an experience for kids and teenagers, you are probably creating content for seven different segments of your time together.

By identifying the segments of every experience, Orange curriculum provides resources that will elevate the quality of what happens in every ministry regardless of your church model, size, style, budget, or location.

SEVEN SEGMENTS OF A WEEKLY EXPERIENCE

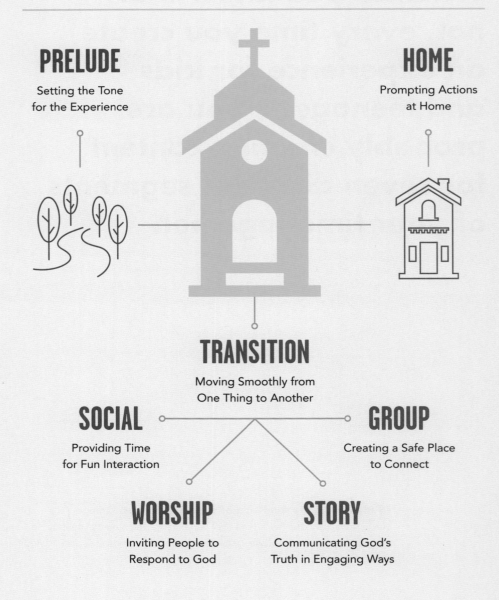

PRELUDE
Setting the Tone
for the Experience

HOME
Prompting Actions
at Home

TRANSITION
Moving Smoothly from
One Thing to Another

SOCIAL
Providing Time
for Fun Interaction

GROUP
Creating a Safe Place
to Connect

WORSHIP
Inviting People to
Respond to God

STORY
Communicating God's
Truth in Engaging Ways

PRELUDE

Setting the Tone for the Experience

It's important for your core **message** to be amplified by your environment. What someone sees, hears, and experiences as they enter into your spaces can reinforce what you want them to remember. First impressions from volunteers or other kids who are **serving** can create a positive and welcoming atmosphere.

Orange curriculum helps set the tone for each week with resources that create an environment on-site including monthly posters, background playlists, original music and music videos, and suggestions for decorating your space to coordinate with a monthly theme.

SOCIAL

Providing Time for Fun Interaction

Fun is essential if you want to influence kids and teenagers. Fun establishes connection. We all tend to learn more from people who we believe actually like us. Establishing a time to simply enjoy being together enhances the potential of **relationships**.

All Orange curriculums provide an activity or game to help kids laugh and connect at the beginning of their time together. The social segment of the curriculum will also connect with the message for the day so it sets the stage for what comes next.

TRANSITION

Moving Smoothly from One Thing to Another

Attention span varies from phase to phase as kids and youth grow, but it's never as long as most of us think it should be. Thinking through programming so segments transition effectively will keep kids or youth from getting distracted and disconnecting from the core ideas of the **message**.

Orange operates on the philosophy that something needs to change about every five minutes if you want to keep kids and teenagers engaged. That's why transitions (as you move from Bible teaching to worship to activities) are so important. Orange curriculum guides leaders through these transitions by scripting what to say as well as offering audio and video cues.

STORY

Communicating God's Truth in Engaging Ways

The most important segment of weekly experiences is the actual Bible story or **message**. Knowing your audience is as important as knowing the Scriptural text. It's important to craft language and use tools to engage the heart and mind of kids at each phase.

Each age-group curriculum provides weekly teaching scripts for communicators to present a relevant and memorable **message**. The teaching scripts are supported with editable graphics, motion graphics, and videos to either support or supplement a live communicator.

WORSHIP

Inviting People to Respond to God

Worship is something we do daily through how we live our lives for God. When we invite youth to pray, give, and even sing together it elevates the idea of loving and honoring God.

Orange preschool and children's curriculum provide an original song every month that corresponds to the monthly theme. All age group curriculums supply song suggestions and resources to help **leaders** engage kids in a musical response to God.

GROUP

Creating a Safe Place to Connect

While the Story segment is the hub of the Bible teaching moment in every weekly experience, the Group segment is where discipleship really happens. Always remember that spiritual formation takes place when **relationships** are a priority. Never economize on time or focus for this part of your environment. Group is where kids and teenagers develop their spiritual habits, language, and perspectives.

Orange age-group curriculums provide leaders with small group resources that reinforce Biblical teaching through activities and conversation guides.

HOME

Prompting Action at Home

When the core messages that you are handing kids are reinforced at home, they will make a different kind of impact. Actually, when families discover concepts and truths together, they can change the home dynamic forever. There is simply no substitute for what can happen in families when they have faith conversations. It has the potential to impact their future relationships like nothing else can.

Orange curriculum provides tools to partner with **parents** in every age group. Parent Cue resources offer age-appropriate tips to help parents be better parents, and to connect parents with what was taught each week. They provide suggestions for leveraging routine family times, such as morning time, drive time, mealtime, or bedtime to make them easy to use at home. There are also Parent Cue digital opportunities for churches to customize, like the Parent Cue App.

5 CRITICAL SHIFTS

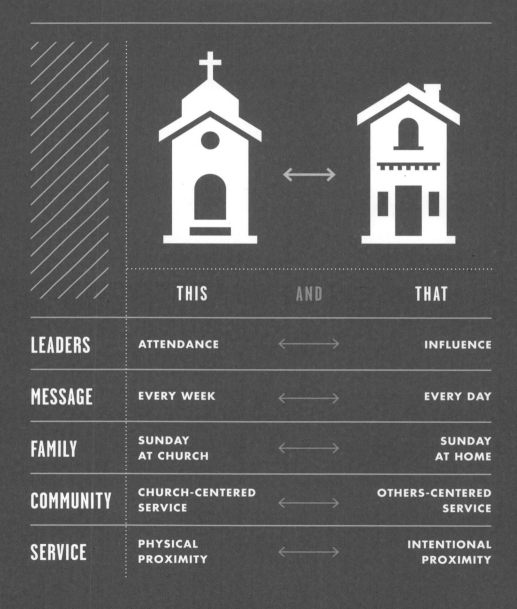

	THIS	AND	**THAT**
LEADERS	ATTENDANCE	⟷	INFLUENCE
MESSAGE	EVERY WEEK	⟷	EVERY DAY
FAMILY	SUNDAY AT CHURCH	⟷	SUNDAY AT HOME
COMMUNITY	CHURCH-CENTERED SERVICE	⟷	OTHERS-CENTERED SERVICE
SERVICE	PHYSICAL PROXIMITY	⟷	INTENTIONAL PROXIMITY

FIVE CRITICAL SHIFTS

Let's recap the idea of change and values for the sake of context.

As **leaders** you have to keep adjusting your yardsticks to clarify what a win looks like. When it comes to your **message**, you will need to rethink your style, technique, media, and platform to keep connecting where and how this generation listens. Although the influence of **family** will always be significant, the picture of family continues to shift in culture. The more you understand the unique needs of family, the better you will be able to influence the homes that shape the future of a generation. It's also important to be students of the everyday culture where kids and teenagers live. The community of consistent leaders and **relationships** we connect to the next generation has to be intentional about understanding a kid's everyday experiences. If we engage in their world then maybe we can earn the right to help them discover their purpose in loving and **serving** their world for the sake of the Gospel.

So, let's revisit the five timeless values that we've highlighted in light of some critical shifts we need to continue to make.

LEADERSHIP

We need to shift from growing **attendance** to include expanding **influence**. Leaders need to create new yardsticks that measure beyond the Sunday morning numbers. It will be important over the next few years for staffs to gauge how a church is growing in its relationship with the community and families outside the church.

MESSAGE

We need to shift from communicating **every week** to include connecting **every day**. A once-a-week message that is not reinforced consistently throughout the week will be crowded out by competing content.

FAMILY

We need to shift from a **"Sunday-at-church"** paradigm to include a **"Sunday-at-home"** mindset. Moving into this decade fewer families will be showing up at church on Sunday, and families who show up will show up less frequently. While Sunday-at-church programming is still important, we will need creative alternatives for a host of families who still want a strategy to influence their kids' faith and character.

COMMUNITY

We need to shift from **physical proximity** to include **intentional proximity**. Simply being in the same physical space does not guarantee the kind of learning, interaction, and change that needs to happen in lives. We have to be more intentional than ever before to build healthy and meaningful friendships. It also means we will need better tools to engage with diverse points of views and to leverage technologies to enhance productive conversations.

SERVICE

We need to shift from **church-centered service** to include **others-centered service**. Weekly opportunities at church can be a training ground for kids and youth to discover and develop their gifts and skills. But if you want to inspire them with a lasting sense of purpose, give them something to do that helps their community outside the church. Better yet, partner with other churches to do meaningful service in a community so kids have a sense of the bigger mission of following Jesus.

As you innovate and reimagine "how" to do ministry, keep coming to "why." When you establish timeless values like these they can be a catalyst and guide as you create a healthy and effective family ministry.

ESSENTIAL

3

ANCHOR THE EVERYDAY FAITH OF KIDS AND TEENAGERS TO WHAT JESUS SAID AND DID

If we could convince a generation to trust Jesus every day, it would transform their capacity to love God, others, and themselves.

Everyday *faith* is another way of saying everyday *trust*.

That's why discipleship starts by inviting others to discover and trust what Jesus said and did. In our Bible story videos, we often say, "It's in the story of God that we can discover the character of God." We could also say, "It's in the story of Jesus that we discover the character of God."

We simply want to anchor kids and teenagers at every phase to what Jesus said and did.

JESUS

As they engage with the story of God, we hope they will begin to . . .
trust what Jesus said about being God.

Jesus actually said, "If you have seen me, you have seen God." This may have seemed a little radical at first, but then He died and came back to life. In other words, if Jesus pulled off the resurrection, then maybe Jesus can be trusted about His claims to be God.

It means we can also . . .
trust what Jesus said about what He said.

Jesus wasn't vague at all about *why* what He said matters. He actually stated,

> "Everybody who hears these words of mine and puts them into practice is like a wise builder who built a house on a rock." Matthew 7:24

Jesus continues in this passage to explain that *everybody* who practices what He says will be able to weather the storms of life. According to Jesus, not only does what He says matter, but it matters to do what He says.

If that's true, then it makes sense to . . .
trust what Jesus said is most important.

It seems reasonable that if Jesus, who was God, said we should build our life around what He said, then whatever Jesus said matters most, actually matters most.

So, what did Jesus say mattered most? Loving God.

When the Pharisees tested Jesus' knowledge of Scripture, they asked this question, "Teacher, which is the greatest commandment in the

Law?" It's interesting what Jesus did *not* say. He *didn't* reply, "All of God's commandments have equal importance." Instead, He actually prioritized truth. Jesus responded by quoting Moses, "The greatest commandment is to love the Lord your God with all of your heart, and with all of your soul, and with all of your strength. This is the first and greatest commandment."

Just in case this idea seems a little overwhelming, Jesus did something to clarify what it looks like to love God. He attached a short, obsolete commandment to the greatest commandment to give more context. Jesus continued . . .

"And the second is like it: Love your neighbor as yourself. There is no commandment greater than these."

Jesus makes a clear connection between loving God and loving others. He even suggests it is normal and natural to love yourself. There's an implied hierarchy in the Great Commandment. Love God, then love others, then love you.

It's as if Jesus is suggesting, "If you want to know if you love God, then look at how you love the people God loves."

As if that's not enough, Jesus makes a point to be sure the crowd understands how important this idea really is. He explains to the Old Testament scholars, "*All* the law and prophets hang on these two commandments." Wait. There is that word "all" again.

Jesus summarizes everything with one concept. He organizes the writings of Moses and the prophets, the major commandments, and the sacred text of the Holy Scriptures **into one overarching idea**.

So, if we trust *what* Jesus said matters most, then we should probably trust *why* Jesus said it matters. According to Jesus, these two commandments are the organizing themes for the rest of Scripture. If the Bible were an epic movie, then it would seem that God the Creator of the world assumed the role of executive producer, cast Jesus as the lead, and wove love as the primary theme throughout the narrative.

THE GREATEST COMMANDMENT

LOVE

**LOVE THE LORD
YOUR GOD WITH ALL
YOUR HEART,
SOUL, AND MIND**

**LOVE
YOUR NEIGHBOR
AS
YOURSELF**

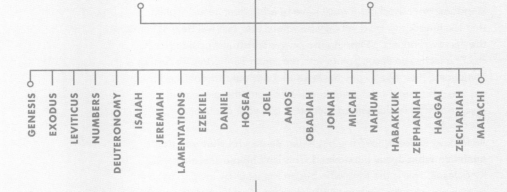

GENESIS · EXODUS · LEVITICUS · NUMBERS · DEUTERONOMY · ISAIAH · JEREMIAH · LAMENTATIONS · EZEKIEL · DANIEL · HOSEA · JOEL · AMOS · OBADIAH · JONAH · MICAH · NAHUM · HABAKKUK · ZEPHANIAH · HAGGAI · ZECHARIAH · MALACHI

**ALL THE LAW AND PROPHETS HANG
ON THESE TWO COMMANDMENTS**

MATTHEW 22:37-40

It's as if Jesus was saying to the Pharisees, "You have been reading the text all wrong. You have been so preoccupied trying to interpret the law that you missed the main point. This isn't about knowing something, it's about loving someone." In Jesus' response to the question about the Greatest Commandment, Jesus not only emphasized the *value* of Scripture, He clarified the *focus* of Scripture.

The emphasis on loving God and others was not a new or isolated focus. Jesus launched His ministry inviting everyone who followed Him to imagine a different kind of Kingdom characterized by God's love. Jesus' teaching was a radical shift from the theological mindset of an entire ancient Hebrew culture.

Interestingly enough, the Pharisees had studied the same law and prophets that Jesus studied, and had arrived at very different conclusions. It seemed unlikely that Jesus was the promised Messiah the Hebrew nation had imagined. They were expecting a conquering King, a warrior Messiah who would defeat their enemies and overturn an oppressive government. It seems reasonable, given their status, that they would have high standing in the legitimate Messiah's new kingdom. How shocking it must have been to hear Jesus explain that His Kingdom would actually be where the "last will be first" and the "first will be last." Flipping the power constructs upside down didn't exactly win Jesus points with the ruling Sanhedrin. To further complicate their rise to power, Jesus had not only admonished them to "love your neighbor,"Jesus suggested something even more revolutionary. He challenged them to "love your enemies."

According to Jesus, love is a big issue. **Be careful that you don't minimize what Jesus maximized.** This isn't hippie Jesus. This is King Jesus. This is the King who began His reign by inviting us to reimagine the value system of His kingdom. And if what Jesus said doesn't build a compelling enough case about the importance of love, then certainly what Jesus did should settle the debate. If we anchor this generation's faith to the Gospel, then maybe we can convince teenagers and kids to . . .

trust what Jesus said because of what Jesus actually did.

Love was not something Jesus simply taught. Love was something Jesus did. The essence of the Gospel story is the fact that God became human to redeem humans. Jesus lived and loved in the tension of humanity. He healed the sick. He publicly forgave sin. He went to parties. He made friends with "sinners." He confronted religious abuse. He elevated the worth of women and children. He prioritized for the poor. He washed the feet of His own disciples.

When Jesus explained,

> "A new commandment I give to you, that you love one another as I have loved you . . . "

His closest followers knew what He meant. They had experienced His love every day.

When Jesus said,

> "Greater love has no one than this: to lay down one's life for one's friends,"

He proved it by dying on a cross for His friends.

When a resurrected Jesus asked Peter for the third time, "Do you love me?," Peter replied, "Lord, you know all things. You know that I love you." Jesus simply responded, "Take care of my sheep."

In other words, "If you really love me, then love the people I love." Of course, it was logical for Peter to tell Jesus, "Lord, you know all things." It's probably what any of us would have said to Jesus after He died and came back to life. The resurrection made what Jesus said even more profound.

According to Jesus, love really matters.

But not just any kind of love. God's love.

The kind of love God proved throughout the history of humanity
The kind of love that created humans in God's image
The kind of love that gave context to the entire law and prophets

The kind of love the angels celebrated
The kind of love Jesus demonstrated
The kind of love that characterizes God's kingdom
The kind of love that went to a cross
The kind of love death couldn't stop
The kind of love God's Spirit keeps nudging in us
The kind of love that is the distinctive mark of being a disciple
The kind of love echoed by every "one another" commandment in
the New Testament

It's the kind of love Jesus wanted the human world to know.
It's the kind of love that Jesus called the human church to show.

It's redeeming love.
It's perfect love.
It's unconditional love.
It's forever love.

No one is suggesting you can actually love perfectly.
You won't get this right.
You can't. Not in this lifetime.
But as long as you are made in the image of God
you are expected to be a light
wherever you can,
whenever you can,
as much as you can.

This kind of love is not superficial, or shallow, or soft. It's actually
supernatural, stubborn, and sacrificial. This kind of love doesn't
compromise truth, or ignore injustice, or refuse to act. God's love
doesn't look the other way. It stares down evil wherever it shows up.
It shows up to forgive when it makes no sense. It steps into the mess
regardless of what it might cost.

TURN LOVE UP

Elevating God's love in your messaging should come with this warning:

Love usually requires change.

Whenever you turn the volume up on love, it almost always threatens existing conditions. When Jesus clarified love as the Greatest Commandment, it forced every other commandment to be re-examined by a higher standard. For those who are comfortable with the way things are, positioning love as a priority can be extremely unsettling.

It's why Jesus stepped into the spotlight declaring, "Your righteousness should exceed the righteousness of the Pharisees." Love always requires more than the definition of the Law. The problem is the religious elite found their identity in the Law. They liked their definitions. They knew how to measure others and found meaning in keeping their rules.

But when Jesus elevated "loving your neighbor" as the standard, it set off alarms. It was like pulling a thread that held their neatly defined theology intact. So, the Pharisees did what Pharisees do. They tested Jesus with a clarifying question, "Who is my neighbor?" Then Jesus did what He did so often. He told a story, and posed a question back to them. Unfortunately, Jesus' response left them exposed as not-so-nice religious experts. Jesus told a parable that presented an outcast Samaritan as responsible and the insider Jewish religious elite as negligent. It certainly must have raised a question for a smart Pharisee, "How can someone who is theologically wrong love God better than someone who is theologically right?"

The Samaritans were the enemy.
The Samaritans were a different ethnic mix.
The Samaritans were theologically inferior.

How could a Samaritan possibly be the hero in a story about
God's love?
Wait.

Actually, the Samaritan wasn't just the hero of the story.
The Samaritan was the *neighbor*!

When Jesus implied the Samaritan was the hero *and* the neighbor, it
put the Pharisees in a predicament. Up until that point, a neighbor
was considered in Hebrew culture as an insider. A neighbor was
someone who lived near you and believed like you. The Pharisees'
reputations as religious leaders were built on a construct that isolated
them from "sinners." Their status in the religious community was
tied to their practice of not associating with people who didn't think,
believe, or look like them.

But in the story about the Good Samaritan, Jesus turned the tables
on the Pharisees—this time figuratively. The "love your neighbor"
imperative created a dilemma. Jesus publicly exposed a flaw in their
separatist ideology. He closed the gap between the self-righteous
Pharisees and the average sinner. The Pharisees were skilled at
manipulating Scriptures to secure their place in Hebrew culture as
experts in the Law. It makes sense that when Jesus turned the volume
up on love, the religious elite got nervous.

The Pharisees knew how to navigate a theology built on the Law,
but not so much on love. They had figured out how to use the Law
as a stepping stone in hierarchy of religious power. Jesus had just
replaced the foundation. Jesus was challenging the process and
complicating the roles they knew how to play. It shouldn't be a
surprise they were having an identity crisis. It makes sense that they
began to scheme to kill Jesus.

Unfortunately, love still threatens religious and theological mindsets.
Maybe that's because there's a little Pharisee that exists in all of
us. We love our certainty, and our clarity, and our codes. But Jesus
rearranged our code and clarified one certainty that has the potential
to change how we see everything and everyone. The point is, when it
comes to talking about God's love we need to keep the volume up,

because Jesus did. And if we hope to disciple an everyday faith that is anchored to what Jesus said and did, love has to be a priority.

The Great Commandment was not simply a way of restating God's laws. Jesus was reprioritizing what mattered most. It's one thing to believe that "All Scripture is equally *inspired* by God," but it's not accurate to claim that "All Scripture is equally *important*." Even Pharisees would agree that all truth is not created equal but they apparently didn't agree with what Jesus prioritized. Jesus didn't make what they wanted to matter matter as much as they wanted it to matter.

Jesus didn't turn the volume up on their
religious authority,
theological expertise,
or righteous living.
He turned the volume up on *love*.

It's possible that few leaders really understood what existed between Jesus and the Pharisees better than Paul. He was a defender of the Law, a Pharisee who persecuted, imprisoned, and killed the followers of Jesus. But this is what he said after his conversion to Christianity,

"I pray that your love will have deep roots. I pray that it will have a strong foundation. May you have power together with all the Lord's holy people to understand Christ's love. May you know how wide and long and high and deep it is. And may you know his love, even though it can't be known completely. Then you will be filled with everything God has for you." Ephesians 3:17-19

Paul's view of the power of God's love to transform someone was as radical then as it is now. There is enough vision in this one passage to explain why love matters so much. Paul prayed for a generation to have "love" with "deep roots" and a "strong foundation." He prayed

THE ORGANIZING IDEA

Love the Lord your
GOD
with all of your
heart, soul, and strength
Love your
NEIGHBOR
as
YOURSELF

WONDER

DISCOVERY

PASSION

Love
God

Love
Life

Love
Others

their love would continue to grow in the context of an authentic faith community so they would know how "wide and long and high and deep" the love of Jesus really is. Paul suggested spiritual growth starts with the love of Jesus and as we grow we keep discovering how to love and be loved by God. Paul even said you don't have to completely understand it to do something about it. Then he hinted at the impact God's love can have on someone's future, ". . . then you will be filled with everything God has for you."

What if we decided as churches to participate in that kind of strategy for the next generation? What if one of our primary goals is to help kids and teenagers "imagine" how big God's love really is? What if we can build the foundation of an everyday faith on God's love in Christ?

THE ORGANIZING IDEA

The obvious application is to leverage the Great Commandment as a basis for *how* and *what* we teach. That's why we try to organize our message around how Jesus suggested truth should be organized. We want to help kids and teenagers . . .

Love God
Love Life
Love Others

We also believe when kids learn to love God,
it will influence their future in a positive way.

When kids love God, it leads to a deeper faith.
When kids love God, it leads to loving others.
When kids love others, it leads to stronger relationships.
When kids love God, it leads to loving themselves.
When kids love themselves, it leads to wiser decisions.

That's why everything we teach comes back to these three relational motives. Our strategy is simply to keep turning these three dials in unique ways at every phase of a kid's life. With that in mind, how would you organize core Scriptural insights in a way that could help kids know how to trust and love God?

If you were to draw three columns to represent the three dials, the first column could represent how kids see God. We refer to it as the "Wonder" dial. The second dial represents how kids see themselves. We refer to it as the "Discovery" dial. And the third dial represents how they see others. We refer to it as the "Passion" dial. To state it another way we simply want to . . .

Incite Wonder about God
Provoke Discovery about Life
Fuel Passion about Others

This helps us as a team organize key truths that we know kids and teenagers will need to keep coming back to over and over again. It's one of the reasons our curriculums are built around what we call a scope and cycle. Creating a cycle to revisit these insights consistently helps kids and teenagers rediscover their meaning at each stage of life. One or more of these nine insights are reflected in each weekly bottom line that is crafted for our age-group curriculums.
We never claim that what we have created is exhaustive. You can make your own list or customize ours. This list of core insights is not intended to be an all-encompassing statement of faith. It is designed to complement the specific statements of faith of the churches and denominations who partner with us.

NINE CORE INSIGHTS

INCITE WONDER ABOUT GOD

I am created to pursue an
authentic relationship with my Creator.

DESIGN of God's Creation
The physical world around us implies the existence of an invisible Creator. The wonders that exist in nature and science reveal an all-powerful God who created the universe with meaning and purpose.

The Genesis story also indicates that people were elevated in Creation to both reflect the image of God and to manage a world God entrusted to their care.

Core Insight: What I see around me reveals a Creator who cares about me.

IDENTITY based on God's Image

Humans were made in the image of God and therefore created with inherent value and worth. Although the image of God was distorted in all humankind as a result of sin, every human has potential to love, reason, create, dream, lead, relate, trust, believe, improve, and reflect God's image.

Core Insight: I am created in the image of God and have unique potential and worth.

CONNECTION because of God's Love

Scripture is clear in indicating that God loved us even though we are sinners. The story of the Bible is a narrative about God pursuing a relationship with us. God's love for us is the reason that we are called to love each other. Jesus clarified that God's love is also the distinctive that characterizes those who follow Him. "We love, because He first loved us."

Core Insight: I live in pursuit of an infinite God who desires an eternal relationship with me.

PROVOKE DISCOVERY ABOUT LIFE

I belong to Jesus Christ and define who I am by what He says.

FAITH in God's Son

The essence of the Gospel message is that Jesus was God born as a human. He died for our sins, and was raised back to life. Jesus stated that He was God and that He had been given all authority over heaven and earth. Jesus also promised those who trust and follow Him that will live with Him forever one day in Heaven. He claimed that He came to give us "life and life more complete."

Core Insight: I believe in Jesus and will continue to trust Him even when life doesn't make sense.

TRANSFORMATION by the power of God's Spirit

Jesus promised that God's Spirit would continue to guide, comfort, teach, and transform us as humans to be more like Jesus. As followers of Jesus, we can have the confidence to know that we are never alone. God's Spirit is always present in our lives to nudge us in the direction of thinking, serving, living, and loving like Christ. The virtues or spiritual qualities that God is cultivating in our lives as Christians include love, joy, peace, resilience, kindness, generosity, faith, humility, and self-control.

Core Insight: God's Spirit is transforming my unique and imperfect life into the character of Jesus.

TRUTH according to God's Message

Jesus' human life, death, and resurrection proved that He is the Messiah who the ancient Hebrew Scriptures had prophesied. Jesus leveraged His authority as God to validate Scripture as authoritative for the Christian life and faith. Jesus also predicted and authenticated the work God would do through the apostles in writing the Gospels and the New Testament. What Jesus clarified by defining the Great Commandment establishes a Scriptural priority to love God and love your neighbor.

Core Insight: What Jesus said and did impacts how I should respond to God's Word in my everyday life.

FUEL PASSION FOR OTHERS

<u>I exist every day to demonstrate
God's love to a broken world.</u>

RESTORATION through participating in God's Story
The Gospel is good news for everyone. Understanding the healing
and restorative message of Jesus for humanity should offer hope
to everyone in the world. His promise offers belonging, freedom,
purpose, forgiveness, and healing to anyone. We are invited to follow
and trust Jesus to become a part of a spiritual movement that shares
the hope of the Gospel, as we love and serve those around us.

**Core Insight: I am designed to participate in God's story
to restore a broken and hurting world.**

COMPASSION that reflects God's Character
Jesus was fully human and fully God. He encountered the same
temptations, emotions, and struggles that humans experience, and
yet never sinned. His life and death indicated that God deeply cares
about the pain and suffering of humanity. What Jesus did on the cross
is evidence that God was willing to become human to prove He fully
understands loneliness, pain, rejection, loss, trauma, guilt, injustice,
even death. God can be trusted to know what we feel, because God
became one of us.

**Core Insight: My faith in Christ is revealed by my compassion and
care for others.**

COMMUNITY in the context of God's Family
The Creation story reveals that humans were designed to be in a
relationship with God and each other. The essence of the Gospel
message is that Jesus' sacrificial death made it possible for humans
to be reconciled with God and each other. When Jesus presented
the concept of the Church to His disciples, He was challenging them
to reimagine a spiritual family that included every nation. Jesus also
predicted that His Church would prevail throughout history and

NINE CORE INSIGHTS

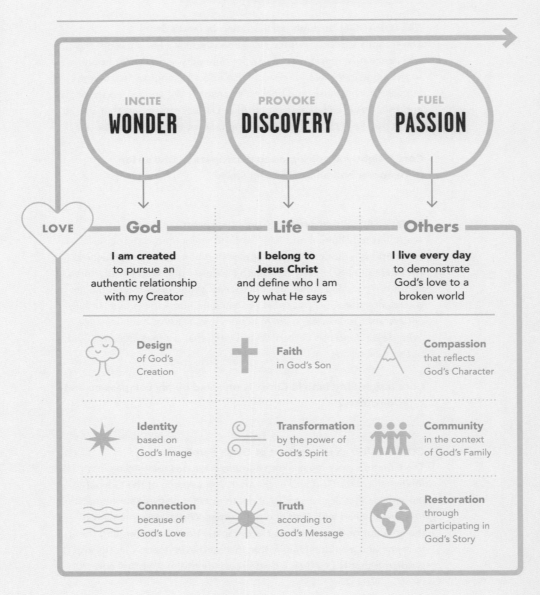

INCITE
WONDER

PROVOKE
DISCOVERY

FUEL
PASSION

LOVE — God — Life — Others

I am created
to pursue an
authentic relationship
with my Creator

**I belong to
Jesus Christ**
and define who I am
by what He says

I live every day
to demonstrate
God's love to a
broken world

Design
of God's
Creation

Faith
in God's Son

Compassion
that reflects
God's Character

Identity
based on
God's Image

Transformation
by the power of
God's Spirit

Community
in the context
of God's Family

Connection
because of
God's Love

Truth
according to
God's Message

Restoration
through
participating in
God's Story

become a force to overcome evil in this world. The church is not a building where people gather, the Church is actually people who gather to worship and follow Jesus.

Core Insight: I choose to live in the complexities of family and community because God values them.

THE PRIORITY

We don't want this generation to miss what Jesus said is most important. If Jesus clearly prioritized loving God, then so should we. Most Christian leaders already intuitively know that Christianity is about a relationship. Discipleship has never been simply about information or beliefs, it's about a relationship with Jesus. It's just too easy to define discipleship as a class or course, not a relational process. From time to time, we need to reset and restart to stay focused on making relationships the priority of our content.

Think about it this way. One day when your kids walk away from your home or church into their adult world, what are a few things you hope will always be true about their faith?

Do you want them to . . .
- → know the names of the twelve disciples?
- → list the books of the Bible?
- → believe what you do about baptism?
- → attend the same denomination?
- → quote your doctrinal statement?
- → define sanctification?
- → follow the Ten Commandments?

What if you actually had to prioritize what you think is most important? What makes the list? Does it mean we shouldn't teach those things? Not at all. It just means we keep organizing what we teach around love. More specifically, around what Jesus said and did related to how He loved us and how He taught us to love.
Isn't it true that you want the kids who grow up in your home or ministry to keep growing in how they trust Jesus? Your hope is that

they will become adults who continue to love God in a way that changes how they love others—including themselves.

The sobering truth is someone can keep the commandments and still be a jerk. You can raise kids that are Biblically literate, but who never demonstrate the fruit of God's Spirit. You can hand faith to a generation that will "move mountains," but without love it will be meaningless. *Didn't Paul say exactly that?*

There's an important premise here related to spiritual growth.

How you trust God affects how you love God.
How you love God affects how you trust God.
How you love God affects how you love others.
How you love others affects how you love God.

When we wrote the book *It's Just a Phase, So Don't Miss It*, we included a Life Map similar to the diagram in this section that connects child development to the concept of faith development. The research we did for this project helps parents and leaders understand the internal crisis that affects a kid's identity at each phase of his or her life. It's based on the simple idea that learning to discover and trust who God is at every phase can give someone a greater sense of identity, belonging, and purpose.

FAITH & CHARACTER

When Jesus confronted the Pharisees with a version of theology that makes "loving your neighbor" a priority, He taught that faith moves us to do something good. His message raised a practical question about the role that faith plays in shaping our character. The context of the story about the Good Samaritan suggests we all have the potential to reflect something about God's character. The interaction with the Pharisees signals to all of us that knowing and loving God should influence us to do good.

Think about what happened:
- ➡ A Pharisee approached Jesus with a theological dilemma.

- Jesus told a story about a Samaritan who stopped to help a hurting man.
- Then Jesus asked a question to prompt the Pharisee to think.
- When the religious leader gave a logical response, Jesus said, "Go do what He did."

Jesus understood how humans learn.

TRUTH + CREATIVITY + CRITICAL THINKING + APPLICATION = RELEVANCE

By the way, Jesus' technique worked. The story of the Good Samaritan stuck. It is one of the most quoted and remembered stories of all time. But knowing the story is not enough. Jesus said, "If you hear these words of mine and do not put them into practice, it's like building your house on sand." He used this metaphor to describe what it looked like to live by His Kingdom virtues.

If you noticed, we just used the word "virtue." That was intentional. There are so many terms we could use when we talk about demonstrating God's love to others. Depending on your experience or circles, some of these terms may have baggage. Words like morals, principles, character, values, and virtues can actually be used to label what is sometimes derogatively referred to as "behavior-based" teaching.

But we believe the goal of teaching should never be just to change behavior, but to influence motive. It's always important to make a clear connection between what we do and why we do it. **Trusting God's character moves us to demonstrate God's character.**

We define a virtue as **"something God is doing in us to change the world around us."** Virtues—at least by the way we define them—start with God. When we talk about character or virtues we are

PHASE LIFE MAP

EVERY KID →

MADE IN THE IMAGE OF GOD

THINKS LIKE AN ARTIST

THINKS LIKE A SCIENTIST

| Am I safe? | Am I able? | Am I okay? | Do I have your attention? | Do I have what it takes? | Do I have friends? |

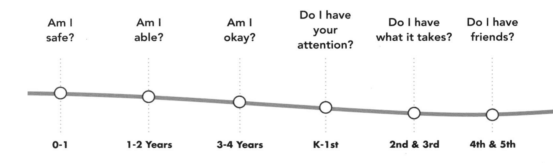

| 0-1 | 1-2 Years | 3-4 Years | K-1st | 2nd & 3rd | 4th & 5th |

Embrace their physical needs

Engage their interests

| To Know God's Love | To Meet God's Family | To Trust God's Character | To Experience God's Family |

Wonder
Discovery
Passion

Wonder
Discovery
Passion

PHASE LIFE MAP (CONTD.)

TO LOVE GOD WITH ALL THEIR HEART, SOUL, AND STRENGTH AND TRUST JESUS → **BETTER FUTURE**

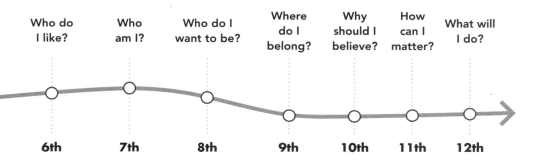

MIDDLE SCHOOL
THINKS LIKE AN ENGINEER

HIGH SCHOOL
THINKS LIKE A PHILOSOPHER

Who do I like?	Who am I?	Who do I want to be?	Where do I belong?	Why should I believe?	How can I matter?	What will I do?
6th	7th	8th	9th	10th	11th	12th

Affirm their personal journey

Mobilize their potential

To Own Their Own Faith	To Value A Faith Community	To Keep Pursuing Authentic Faith	To Discover A Personal Mission

Wonder
Discovery
Passion

Wonder
Discovery
Passion

always referring to concepts that we believe are "rooted in love" for God. Virtues should never be positioned or taught in the context of earning credit with God, or the way to find redemption. Virtues are simply a **reflection of** or a **response to** the character of God.

Remember two things:
1. Every human was created in the **image of God**.
2. Every Christian is being transformed by the **Spirit of God**.

We are not made like God, but we are made in the likeness of God. There is amazing potential in all of us.

A parent who loves a child is reflecting the image of God.
A teenager doing a service project is reflecting the image of God
Any leader confronting evil or injustice is reflecting the image of God.
Jesus, the Son of God, said,
> "Let your light shine in front of others so they can see your good works and glorify your Father which is in Heaven."

By the way, Jesus said this to everyone in the crowd regardless of what they believed.

The question for leaders and parents is never, "*Are* you going to teach character or virtues to kids and teenagers?" But rather, "*How* are you going to teach character to kids and teenagers?"

Every adult is automatically teaching character to kids whether they know it or not. We teach character by what we say, what we ask, how we respond, and how we treat those around us. One primary question we need to ask is, "How does faith influence how we teach kids and teenagers about character or virtues?" Every kid and teenager should understand they are made in the image of God with a capacity to love, and think, and grow in how they reflect the likeness of God. Responding to God's character in practical ways is also a matter of faith. *When we fail to lead kids to understand spiritual virtues, we choose to hand them an ineffective and irrelevant faith.*

The writers of the New Testament evidently believed it was important to connect our faith to what we actually do.

James, the brother of Jesus said,
    "Don't be hearers of the word and not doers."

Paul, the former Pharisee turned Christian said,
    "Don't get tired of doing what is right"

Here's another compelling idea from Hebrews,

"Stir up [provoke, stimulate] one another to love and good works." Hebrews 10:24

What if we just do that?

Every coach, counselor, and psychologist will agree with this Scriptural statement, "Fix your thoughts on what is true, and honorable, and right, and pure, and lovely, and admirable. Think about things that are excellent and worthy of praise."

Scripture insists that we guard our minds by focusing our thoughts on what is good, to replace thoughts that are wrong. Even non-Christian experts know the power of choosing to think about what we should be thinking about. It's not a new idea, it was God's idea. Maybe that's why there are hundreds of passages written by God-inspired people who actually encountered Jesus.

The New Testament writers gave clear instructions on how we should act toward each other. It's almost as if they took Jesus at His Word when He said, "Love each other as I have loved you . . . by this will all people know that you are my disciples, if you have love for one another." When you read through their inspired letters to the church in their day, it seems like they are simply expanding and applying what it looks like to love others. Take your time reading through a few of them.

We should make sure to . . .

- Love one another (John 13:34, and this command occurs at least 16 times)
- Be devoted to one another (Romans 12:10)
- Honor one another above yourselves (Romans 12:10)
- Live in harmony with one another (Romans 12:16)
- Build up one another (Romans 14:19; 1 Thessalonians 5:11)
- Be like-minded towards one another (Romans 15:5)
- Accept one another (Romans 15:7)
- Admonish one another (Romans 15:14, Colossians 3:16)
- Greet one another (Romans 16:16)
- Care for one another (1 Corinthians 12:25)
- Serve one another (Galatians 5:13)
- Bear one another's burdens (Galatians 6:2)
- Forgive one another (Ephesians 4:2, 32; Colossians 3:13)
- Be patient with one another (Ephesians 4:2, Colossians 3:13)
- Be kind and compassionate to one another (Ephesians 4:32)
- Consider others better than yourselves (Philippians 2:3)
- Look to the interests of one another (Philippians 2:4)
- Bear with one another (Colossians 3:13)
- Comfort one another (1 Thessalonians 4:18)
- Encourage one another (1 Thessalonians 5:11)
- Exhort one another (Hebrews 3:13)
- Show hospitality to one another (1 Peter 4:9)
- Pray for one another (James 5:16)

These are just some of the characteristics the church is called to demonstrate and practice. Of course, if you want a shorter list, let's review what Paul actually says the Holy Spirit is at work doing in us.

"But the fruit of the Spirit is love, joy, peace, patience, kindness, goodness, faithfulness, gentleness, and self-control. Against such things there is no law."
Galatians 5:22

It all really does come back to what Jesus said and did. Jesus put an exclamation mark on loving God. Jesus influenced the apostles who knew Him to keep writing about how we should treat each other, and He gave us the Spirit of God to keep nudging us, to empower us, to keep shaping us to become more like Him. If you want a kid or teenager to understand what every day faith looks like, then either of these lists could be a good place to start.

BETTER CONVERSATIONS

Chances are pretty likely that your kids will grow up and develop perspectives that are different than you about a lot of things, including faith. Most kids do. If you fight too hard to win any argument, you can lose their heart. Your kids may concede silently and temporarily, until they walk away. Whatever you talk them into, someone else can talk them out of. Kids and teenagers are like any of the rest of us, they need to process what they are thinking where it's safe to think. We need to learn how to have better conversations where our kids and teenagers can be intellectually honest.

If you are too dogmatic about the wrong things, you could actually hinder someone from talking about the most important things. It's possible that your confident certainty can sabotage someone's discovery. Thought-provoking questions are almost always better than rehearsed answers. It doesn't mean truth isn't absolute, nor does it mean that you shouldn't be absolute about some things. It's just reminds us no one owns absolute rights to all of the truth. Be careful that you don't make your nuanced theological opinions more important than the Gospel of Jesus, or you could actually sabotage someone's faith.

Besides, the Christian faith isn't really an argument to be won, it's a relationship to be pursued. If you are wrong about love, it doesn't matter what you are right about. At least that will be true when it comes to handing the kids and teenagers you love this faith. Truth without love is dangerous. Ask the Pharisees. They struggled with that same mindset. They couldn't see the gap in their theology, and it was a big one. They were more consumed with being right about the law, than they were about being right with their others. That kind of thinking can make your deep theology rather shallow.

Our team works with eighty different denominations. They teach us so many amazing things about theology, and God's love, and the power of the Gospel. There's a possibility we are all wrong about something—especially if you ask the other denominations.

That's okay.

We need each other to disagree about some things. If we disagree then we can prove what unity of purpose looks like.

What if our overarching goal is simply to help every kid and teenager keep trusting Jesus in a way that influences how they love God, others, and themselves?

What if anchoring what they believe to what Jesus said and did builds a more resilient and dynamic faith?

What if how kids and teenagers understand God's love can actually impact how they view themselves?

What if faith in God can shape their sense of identity, belonging, and purpose?

What if the Gospel is big enough for all of us who follow Jesus to have different experiences and opinions and still be part of the same body?

The Gospel is intended to connect a Church of diverse leaders in a such a remarkable way that it continues to convince the rest of the world that Jesus really is who He said He is.

THE ORANGE PROMISE

Orange is a non-profit organization that exists to help parents and churches influence the next generation. We win when you win at what you do.

We will stay focused on what matters most . . .
because the faith and future of a generation is at stake.

We will be developmentally responsible . . .
because kids and teenagers need to be seen at every phase.

We will give you more than you can use . . .
because we know most churches want options.

We will add people to your team . . .
because every Orange Specialists who works here loves churches.

We will respond to every question . . .
because we know you may actually know the answer.

We will keep improving . . .
because we will try some things that don't work.

We will never stop learning . . .
because we are smart enough to know what we don't know.

ORANGE LIFE STAGE CURRICULUMS

Create a better experience for kids and teenagers this week with a comprehensive strategy— from birth to graduation.

Preschool Curriculum

IN THE PRESCHOOL YEARS, A CHILD WILL FORM THEIR FIRST IMPRESSION OF GOD'S LOVE.

God Made Me
God Loves Me
Jesus Wants to Be My Friend Forever

First Look preschool ministry curriculum provides you with the strategy and tools you need to create an engaging, inspiring, and excellent environment to give preschoolers a foundation of faith that will last a lifetime

FirstLookCurriculum.com

Elementary & Preteen Curriculum

IN THE ELEMENTARY YEARS, A CHILD WILL GROW IN WISDOM, FAITH, AND FRIENDSHIP.

I need to make the wise choice.
I can trust God no matter what.
I should treat others the way I want to be treated.

252 Kids and Preteen ministry curriculum weaves together music, communicator scripts, small group discussions, video presentations, and creative activities based on a clear and simple bottom line each week so kids walk away remembering what matters most.

252KidsCurriculum.com

Middle School Curriculum

IN THE MIDDLE SCHOOL YEARS, A PRETEEN WILL BEGIN TO PERSONALIZE AND OWN THEIR OWN FAITH.

I will follow Jesus because He knows me better than myself.
I will love God because He will never stop loving me.
I will live out God's story so others can know who Jesus is.

XP3 Middle School ministry curriculum is more than just sermons and games—though it's got plenty of those, too. It's a strategy designed to speak straight to a middle schooler—and the people who invest in them, too!

XP3MS.com

High School Curriculum

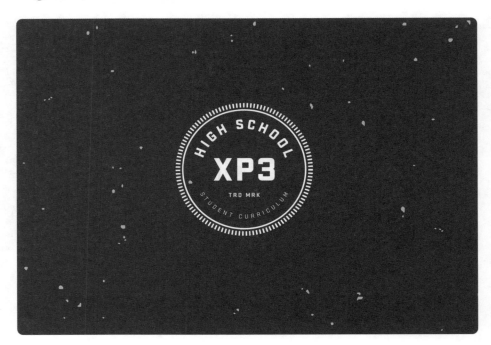

IN THE HIGH SCHOOL YEARS, A TEENAGER WILL DEEPEN AND PERSONALIZE THEIR FAITH IN CHRIST.

**I'm created to pursue a relationship with my Creator.
I trust what Jesus did to transform who I need to become.
I exist to demonstrate God's love to those around me.**

XP3 High School ministry curriculum creates weekly resources to help teenagers experience what God wants to do through them. When you mobilize their potential, students in ninth through twelfth grade will keep pursuing authentic faith and discover a personal mission.

XP3HS.com

ORANGE TRAINING & RESOURCES

Best practices, innovative strategies, and new ideas built around a timeless message.

Orange Members

AN ALL-ACCESS RESOURCE LIBRARY FILLED WITH THE ANSWERS TO THE MINISTRY QUESTIONS YOU ASK MOST.

Customizable resources and exclusive membership-only perks

OrangeMembership.com

Orange Masterclass

MINISTRY TRAINING COURSES FULL OF HIGH-LEVEL INSIGHT AND INNOVATION ON AN ARRAY OF RELEVANT TOPICS.

Innovative Strategies
Engaging Videos
Interactive Workbooks

OrangeMasterclass.com

Parent Cue

**RESOURCES FOR PARENTS
TO HELP YOU BE THE PARENT
YOU WANT TO BE.**

With resources for every parent, grandparent, or caregiver, Parent Cue provides parents at every phase with expert articles, books, courses, and media.

ParentCue.org

OVER 150,000 COPIES SOLD

lead
small.

Five Big Ideas Every
Small Group Leader
Needs to Know

by Reggie Joiner and Tom Shefchunas

A book for every small group
leader on the planet

ORANGESTORE.COM/LEADSMALL

Five questions leaders and volunteers should answer to give every kid hope